Landmark
Events in
American
History

# The
# Trail of Tears

D. L. Birchfield

WORLD ALMANAC® LIBRARY

Please visit our web site at: www.worldalmanaclibrary.com
For a free color catalog describing World Almanac® Library's list of high-quality books and multimedia programs, call 1-800-848-2928 (USA) or 1-800-387-3178 (Canada). World Almanac® Library's fax: (414) 332-3567.

Library of Congress Cataloging-in-Publication Data

Birchfield, D. L., 1948-
    The Trail of Tears / by D. L. Birchfield.
        p. cm. — (Landmark events in American history)
    Summary: Describes the history of the five tribes of Southeastern America, the Cherokee, Chickasaw, Choctaw, Creek, and Seminole, especially their forcible removal in the 19th century to the Great Plains.
    Includes bibliographical references and index.
    ISBN 0-8368-5381-4 (lib. bdg.)
    ISBN 0-8368-5409-8 (softcover)
    1. Trail of Tears, 1838—Juvenile literature.  2. Five Civilized Tribes—Relocation—Juvenile literature.  3. Cherokee Indians—Relocation—Juvenile literature.  4. Indian Territory—History—Juvenile literature.  [1. Trail of Tears, 1838.  2. Five Civilized Tribes—History.  3. Indians of North America—Southern States—History.  4. Indians of North America—Oklahoma—History.]  I. Title.  II. Series.
    E99.C5B483   2003
    973.04'9755—dc21                                              2003047918

First published in 2004 by
**World Almanac® Library**
330 West Olive Street, Suite 100
Milwaukee, WI  53212  USA

Produced by Discovery Books
Editor: Sabrina Crewe
Designer and page production: Sabine Beaupré
Photo researcher: Sabrina Crewe
Maps and diagrams: Stefan Chabluk
World Almanac® Library editorial direction: Mark J. Sachner
World Almanac® Library art direction: Tammy Gruenewald
World Almanac® Library production: Beth Meinholz and Jessica Yanke

Photo credits: Troy Anderson/Native Stock: p. 29; Corbis: pp. 5, 8, 9, 11, 13, 17, 22, 24, 31, 32, 36, 37, 38, 40, 41, 43; Gilcrease Museum, Tulsa, OK: p. 28; The Granger Collection: pp. 30, 35; Native Stock: cover, pp. 4, 6, 27, 34, 42; North Wind Picture Archives: pp. 7, 10, 12, 14, 15, 16, 18, 19, 21, 23, 25, 33, 39.

Printed in the United States of America

1 2 3 4 5 6 7 8 9 07 06 05 04 03

# Contents

# Introduction

**A Kind Offer**

"Rightly considered, the **policy** of the General Government toward the red man is not only liberal, but generous. He is unwilling to submit to the laws of the States and mingle with their population. To save him from this alternative, or perhaps utter annihilation, the General Government kindly offers him a new home, and proposes to pay the whole expense of his removal and settlement."

*President Andrew Jackson, Second Annual Message to Congress, 1830*

## Rise of the United States

History took a grim turn for the Indians of North America when the British **colonies** broke away from Britain in 1776. The young, weak United States needed Indian military allies until the War of 1812 was over. After that, Indians were no longer necessary to white people, and the swelling white American population was hungry for Indian land. Americans were determined to acquire it by whatever means necessary, including the removal of Native tribes from their homelands.

## The Five Civilized Tribes

The era of Indian removal in the 1830s was one of the darkest periods in the history of five of the North American continent's greatest tribes: the Cherokees, Choctaws, Chickasaws, Seminoles, and Muscogees (also called the Creeks).

These Cherokee dancers are wearing a mixture of western and traditional clothing. Members of the Five Civilized Tribes assumed aspects of western culture, which made them appear more "civilized" to whites.

The tribes, originally based in North America's southeastern region, were known collectively by whites as the Five Civilized Tribes. This was partly because their highly developed social and governmental institutions were the rival of anything that white civilization had to offer. What Native people lacked, however, was a large enough population to match the high numbers of Europeans who moved to North America from the 1500s onward.

## Indian Removal

During removal, the five tribes were forcibly uprooted from their ancestral homelands in the Southeast by the U.S. government and moved hundreds of miles to a place on the edge of the Great Plains. It is now the eastern part of the state of Oklahoma. In the 1830s, about sixty thousand people were forced to leave their homes and make this journey. The death rate along the way was so high that the removals have come to be known as "The Trail of Tears."

**Cruelest Work**

"I fought through the Civil War and have seen men shot to pieces and slaughtered by thousands, but the Cherokee removal was the cruelest work I ever knew."

*A Civil War colonel who had earlier taken part in the Cherokee removal*

5

# The People of the Southeast

This spear point, known as a Clovis point, was used for killing game by Clovis people, early North Americans whose culture existed 10,000–11,000 years ago. Before they began to farm, the people of North America depended on hunting, fishing, and wild plants for their food.

## The First North Americans

During the Ice Age, which took place from about 8,000 to 12,000 years ago, huge glaciers—great bodies of ice—dominated the climate of North America. The glaciers covered most of present-day Canada. It was too cold nearly everywhere on the continent even for trees to grow.

The glaciers began melting about 10,000 years ago. By about 7,500 years ago, trees appeared, and by about 5,000 years ago, vegetation flourished and the climate of North America was as we know it today.

Before the glaciers melted, the Native peoples of North America had been **nomadic** hunters, following herds of big game animals across the treeless plains. When the climate changed, the resulting growth of vegetation allowed people to settle in one area for the first time. No one knows exactly when the ancestors of the Five Civilized Tribes settled in the southeastern portion of North America, but it was certainly several thousand years ago.

## Agriculture

People living in the hotter climate of Central America developed farming much earlier than those in North America. Slowly, over a period of 1,000 to 1,500 years, agriculture spread northward from tribe to tribe, traveling along the trade routes. By about 1500 B.C., corn was being grown in the American Southwest.

By about 1000 B.C., tribes east of the Mississippi River were growing corn. The cultivation of corn and other crops, especially beans and squash, allowed people to become truly settled in permanent villages and towns for the first time.

An agricultural village in what is now North Carolina as depicted in the late 1500s by John White, an artist from England. He shows pumpkins, corn and beans at various stages of the crop cycle.

## Mound Builders

By about 500 B.C., great civilizations, now known as the Mound Builders, began arising in the fertile river valleys of the woodlands east of the Mississippi River. They were the ancestors of the Five Civilized Tribes and of many other tribes in the eastern half of North America.

The Mound Builders built mounds out of dirt, constructing them with one basketful of dirt at a time. At first, the mounds were built as burial mounds. Later, people built **effigy** mounds in the shape of birds or snakes. In time, very large mounds called temple mounds were created that had wooden temples built on top of them.

The mound-building cultures reached their peak in about A.D. 1300. By that time, more than 100,000 mounds had been built in the Mississippi River valley.

# Cahokia

The largest known city of the Mound Builders was Cahokia, and its remains are in Illinois, across the Mississippi River from St. Louis, Missouri. The city was spread over 6 square miles (15 square kilometers). Many big mounds can still be seen there—Cahokia's largest mound had a base bigger than the Great Pyramid of Egypt.

One of the mounds still visible at Cahokia, once a large city.

At its height, which was between A.D. 1100 and 1300, Cahokia was home to about thirty thousand people, making it a city with a population the size of London, England, at the time. People lived under a complex class system, with spiritual leaders at the top, at least one middle class, and a working class of laborers.

Cahokia was at the center of a huge trade network, and in the area around the city there were many smaller towns and farming villages. When European explorers came through in the 1680s, however, all that remained on the site was a small village.

### Decline of the Mound Builders

No one knows why the mound-building cultures declined. Some were still active when Europeans first explored the region, and one small temple mound tribe, the Natchez of the lower Mississippi River valley, survived until its people were destroyed by French colonists in 1731.

The decline of the large, centralized populations of the Mound Builders resulted in the formation of many smaller tribes throughout the eastern woodlands. Very little is known about the people in the region during the centuries after 1300, until European exploration of the region began in the 1500s and 1600s.

## European Contact

Europeans had a great impact on the final decline of the Mound Builders. Even before Europeans had explored the interior of the continent, their contact with Native peoples on the coasts had led to the spread of European diseases along Native trade routes. It has been estimated that those diseases, such as smallpox, killed as much as 90 percent of the Native population of North America—several million people—during the 1500s and 1600s.

By 1700, when Europeans had settled close enough to the tribes in the Southeast to begin becoming acquainted with them, the Natchez were the only remaining temple mound culture still in existence. By that time, however, four of the Five Civilized

The French who explored North America in the 1600s encountered the last of the Mound Builders when they met the Natchez people of the Southeast. This French drawing shows a Natchez Indian.

## Geographical Location of the Tribes

Collectively, the Five Tribes controlled most of southeastern North America. The Choctaws were in present-day Mississippi and a large part of western Alabama. The Chickasaws controlled northern Mississippi, northwestern Alabama, western Tennessee, and western Kentucky. The Cherokees inhabited the southern Appalachian Mountain region of eastern Kentucky, eastern Tennessee, northeastern Alabama, northern Georgia, and western North Carolina. The Muscogees were in western South Carolina, most of Georgia, and much of eastern Alabama. The Seminoles, who broke away from the Muscogees during the 1700s and formed a separate tribe, spread throughout most of Florida after the Native population there had been destroyed by Spanish colonists.

This map was drawn in the 1770s, about sixty years before the removal of the tribes. It shows the homelands and main settlements of the five tribes. The colonies marked here had different boundaries than the present-day states with the same names.

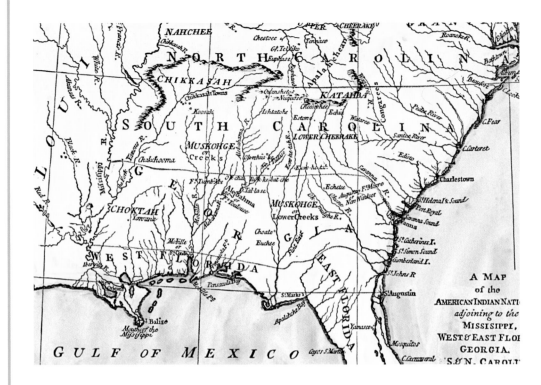

Tribes had settled into their ancestral homelands and had adopted the cultures that would distinguish them.

## Freedom of Speech and Government

Scholars have made comparisons between the political life of the Five Civilized Tribes and that of the ancient **republics** of Greece. One example of the respect for fundamental liberties held among the five tribes is the manner in which freedom of speech was practiced among the Choctaws.

For public debate on the issues of the day, a large brush **arbor** was constructed. The roof, made of tree branches covered with dense leaves, had a hole in the center. Below that hole, through which the full heat of the Mississippi sun beat down on hot days, people who desired to speak were allowed to talk for as long as they could stand in the sun. The Choctaws said they could bear to remain comfortably seated in the shade and listen for as long as the speaker could bear to stand in the sun and speak. They also believed this method taught people to organize their thoughts, say only what needed to be said, and then sit down and shut up.

The tribes divided governmental responsibilities between different villages during times of war and times of peace. Red towns

### A Choctaw Ball Game

"The game commenced with the judges throwing up the ball and firing a gun. An instant struggle ensued between the players, as some six or seven hundred men mutually endeavored to catch the ball in their sticks and throw it into their opponent's goal. Hundreds ran together and leapt over each other's heads, and darted between their adversaries' legs, tripping and throwing and foiling each other in every possible manner. Every voice was raised in shrill yelps and barks. . . . Every trick is used that can be devised, to oppose the progress of the ball. These obstructions often meet desperate resistance, which terminate in a violent scuffle, and sometimes fisticuffs. Sticks are dropped, and the parties are unmolested as they settle it between themselves."

*American painter George Catlin, describing a Choctaw ball game, 1834*

A Chickasaw village once stood on this spot at Natchez Trace, Mississippi. Tribal leadership switched among villages, depending on whether it was a time of peace or a time of war.

## Southeastern Indian Languages

Four of the Five Civilized Tribes speak languages of the Muskogean language family. These include the shared language of the Muscogees and Seminoles and the languages of the Choctaws and Chickasaws (which are nearly identical to each other). The Cherokees, however, speak a language of the Iroquoian language family, which is distantly related to the language of the Mohawks and other Iroquoian tribes of the Northeast, indicating that—in the distant past—the Cherokees separated from their Iroquoian relatives.

In addition to the Five Civilized Tribes, which were large **nations**, there were other, smaller tribes of Native peoples in the southeastern region of the continent, who spoke yet other languages. In order to conduct trade, the southeastern peoples developed a form of communication specifically for that purpose. It was based on the Choctaw and Chickasaw language, but it also borrowed from other languages in the area. It was not a language itself but what is known as a jargon. All the Native peoples of the Southeast knew this jargon, called Mobilian Trade Jargon, and they used it to conduct business with other tribes throughout the region.

were villages that had obligations of leadership during a war. White towns were responsible for leadership in times of peace.

These sorts of institutions distinguished the Five Civilized Tribes in the eyes of others. Europeans recognized that they were people who cherished basic rights and freedoms in a highly cultured society.

## The Role of Women

The civilizations of the Five Civilized Tribes differed greatly from those of Europeans. Perhaps most importantly, women had much more power among these Native peoples.

The Five Civilized Tribes were matrilineal, meaning that descent was traced through the female line. Upon marriage, the husband went to live with the wife's family. Abuses such as wife beating were virtually unknown because women were constantly surrounded by their male relatives. Women owned both the homes they lived in and the agricultural fields. Children of a marriage also automatically belonged to the wife's **clan**. This arrangement avoided child custody disputes in the event of a divorce, because the children always remained with their clan.

These arrangements gave women important roles in their nations. The system was very different from European cultures of the time, in which a married woman was legally the property of her husband and enjoyed few protections from him under the law.

Wilma Mankiller was leader of the Cherokee nation from 1985 to 1995. In Cherokee society, women traditionally were property owners and held power in the commmunity.

# The Coming of the Europeans

Hernando de Soto is greeted by an Indian leader in 1540. The Spanish expedition spread fatal diseases in the area, and de Soto's men killed and enslaved many people.

## Hernando de Soto

For the Native people of the southeastern part of the North American continent, the first prolonged contact with Europeans was the deadly expedition led by Spaniard Hernando de Soto. This began in 1539, a time when most of the mound-building cultures had already declined and many smaller tribes had been formed.

De Soto organized a large military expedition to conquer the Indians of the southeastern region of North America, whom he hoped possessed great wealth in gold. For three years, his men crisscrossed the Southeast, laying waste to villages and taking some Native people as slaves and killing and torturing others. The Spaniards never found any gold, but they set a ruthless precedent of greed and violence for other Europeans to follow.

In northern Mississippi, the Chickasaws set fire to the village that de Soto and his men had seized for their winter quarters, destroying most of his supplies. Greatly weakened, the expedition had to fight its way to the Mississippi River, where de Soto himself was killed in battle in 1542.

## Florida's People Are Destroyed

In 1565, the Spanish established a fort at St. Augustine in Florida. Within 150 years, virtually all of Florida's original Native people had been wiped out by European diseases and slavery and by the brutal colonial warfare that took

place between the Spanish and the English. During the 1700s, bands of Muscogees moved south into the areas of Florida that had been emptied of their Native population. There, they gradually formed a separate tribe that became known as the Seminoles.

## European Trade Goods

The Europeans brought items that Indians had never had before: steel axes, knives and traps, metal pots and pans, firearms, mirrors, ribbons, highly polished beads, and many other things that Indians soon desired. To obtain these things by trade with Europeans, Indians greatly increased their harvest of deer hides and animal furs. In a short time, Native people became dependent on the trade goods and lost much of their **economic** independence. The introduction of European trade brought great changes to the traditional cultures of the tribes. The five large southeastern tribes adapted to those changes very well, which is another reason that Europeans called them the Five Civilized Tribes.

The Spanish gained a permanent foothold in the Southeast with the settlement of St. Augustine, above, founded in Florida in 1565. Soon, the original Indian population in the region had disappeared.

## Pushing into Native Lands

When the English founded the colonies of North and South Carolina in the 1600s, they began making slave raids deep in the Southeast. The late 1600s and early 1700s were a time of terror for the five tribes, who saw many of their people captured by British slave raiders. During the 1700s, the British pushed westward, taking the eastern portions of Cherokee and Muscogee lands to form part of the colony of Georgia.

The French founded Mobile in 1702, on the present-day Alabama coast. This area was on the southeastern edge of the Choctaw country and the southwestern edge of the Muscogee country. In 1718, the French then founded New Orleans, near the mouth of the Mississippi River, on the southwestern edge of the Choctaw country.

As white settlement moved farther south and west, conflict between settlers and Indians grew. This engraving shows a typical battle over territory on the borders of Georgia and the Carolinas.

Before the French were defeated in the French and Indian War, they won several victories against the British with the help of Indian allies. In this drawing, a Native force is ambushing British troops under General Edward Braddock during the French and Indian War.

## Colonial Power Changes Hands

At the end of the French and Indian War (1754–1763), the French were expelled from North America, leaving the British in competition with the Spanish for European control of Native lands in the Southeast. The American Revolution (1776–1783) removed the British, but it also brought a new danger to the Native peoples of North America: an independent American nation, hungry for Indian land.

## The Choctaw Civil War

In order for the Choctaws to obtain French trade goods, the French demanded an exclusive trade alliance. Compared with British trade goods, however, the French items were poorly made, more expensive, and always in short supply. During the 1740s, a Choctaw leader named Red Shoes began urging that the Choctaws get their trade goods from the British in the Carolinas. When Red Shoes brought British traders into the Choctaw country in the late 1740s, the French demanded that the Choctaws put Red Shoes to death. This ignited a civil war among the Choctaws that lasted from 1747 to 1750 and was extremely bloody. Finally, when the Choctaws realized that they were exterminating themselves for the benefit of the Europeans, they ended the civil war, keeping their alliance with the French. But the death toll in their conflict weakened them as a nation for the rest of the eighteenth century.

# Americans Demand Removal

Thomas Jefferson (above) was president of the United States from 1801 to 1809. Like others of his culture and period, he believed that Native Americans should adopt white ways of living or be removed from lands where whites wanted to settle.

## The Beginning of an Idea

Indian removal is an idea associated with President Andrew Jackson because the removals started when he was president of the United States in the 1830s. The idea actually began, however, with President Thomas Jefferson in 1802.

In December 1802 and February 1803, President Jefferson outlined a secret Indian policy in two letters, one to Henry Dearborn, the U.S. secretary of war, and one to William Henry Harrison, governor of Indiana **Territory**. The ideas outlined in those two letters predicted what would happen thirty years later to the southeastern Indians.

## Jefferson's Plan

Jefferson's plan for the Indians had two parts. The first was to encourage the tribes to run up big debts at U.S. trading houses, so that they would have to give up their land to pay the debts. The second part was to populate the Mississippi River region (at that time the western boundary of the United States) with white settlers, so that Indians would be encircled by whites. The settlers eventually would crowd the Indians to such a point that the Indians would be willing to move beyond the Mississippi River to get away from them.

The first tribe that President Jefferson tried to get to move to the land west of the Mississippi was the Choctaws, in 1805. The Choctaws refused even to talk about removal, although they did give up land to pay trading house debts. President Jefferson later changed his mind about Indian removal and stopped pursuing it as a policy in 1808.

## The Louisiana Purchase

An unexpected event in 1803 made Indian removal more achievable. France surprised the United States by offering to sell the Americans the vast territory, then known as Louisiana, west of the Mississippi River. President Jefferson jumped at the offer. Before the year was over, the Americans were in possession of an area that stretched to the Rocky Mountains. Now there was plenty of land to which Native people could be banished.

## Georgia's Claims

At the time, Georgia claimed that its western border extended all the way to the Mississippi River. The United States wanted to create new states in the land that is now the states of Alabama and Mississippi. So on April 23, 1803, President Jefferson paid the state of Georgia $1,250,000 (about $25 million today) for Georgia to give up its claims to that western land.

In 1804, President Jefferson sent his private secretary, Meriwether Lewis, and a soldier, William Clark, to explore the lands west of the Mississippi recently acquired by the United States in the Louisiana Purchase. This picture of Lewis and Clark meeting Native people in Iowa is by Patrick Gass, a member of the expedition.

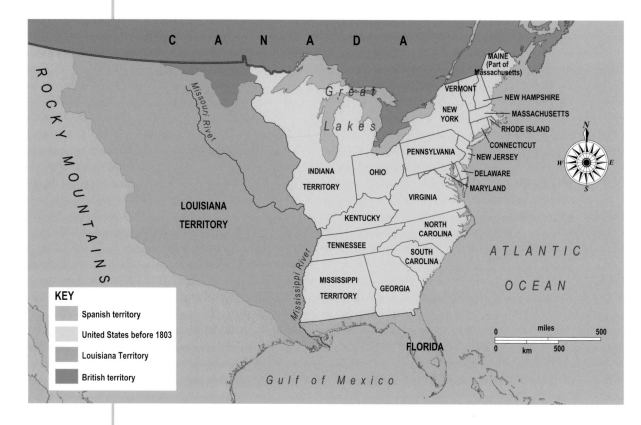

Map Key:

KEY
- Spanish territory
- United States before 1803
- Louisiana Territory
- British territory

By 1800, the United States had pushed its frontier west to the Mississippi River. The Louisiana Purchase of 1803 added over 900,000 square miles (2.3 million sq km) to U.S. territory.

In the same agreement, the U.S. government made a promise to Georgia that would prove fatal for thousands of Native people. The government said it would abolish all other Indian rights to land in Georgia as quickly as possible—this meant Cherokee land in northern Georgia and Muscogee land in western Georgia. Because of this promise, it would be the Georgians clamoring for Indian removal who would put the most pressure on Congress to pass the Indian Removal Act of 1830.

## Tecumseh's Vision

In 1811, Americans on the southern **frontier** were terrified at the threat posed by the great Shawnee warrior Tecumseh, who had a vision for a military alliance of all Indian tribes against the United States. It was other southern Indians, however, who defeated Tecumseh's plans. Chief Pushmataha of the Choctaws vigorously opposed Tecumseh and convinced the Choctaws not to join him. When Tecumseh visited the Muscogees, about half joined him and about half refused.

# Tecumseh (c.1768—1813)

Tecumseh was born into the Shawnee people near what is now Springfield, Ohio. He was a skilled warrior and first fought Americans in 1792. In the early 1800s, he tried to unite many Indian tribes in a military alliance to stop American settlers from taking Indian land west of the Appalachian Mountains. Tecumseh gained a strong following —with thousands of his men, he joined the British to fight white Americans in the War of 1812. Widely known and respected by both sides for his humanity, Tecumseh helped save the lives of white prisoners of war. On October 5, 1813, in the Battle of the Thames in Canada, Tecumseh and his men stood their ground against an American attack while the British retreated. Tecumseh was killed in the attack, and his dream of uniting the Indian tribes died with him.

Tecumseh intervenes to prevent the death of a white man during the War of 1812.

The Battle of New Orleans was the final conflict in the War of 1812. The British were soundly defeated by U.S. troops under Andrew Jackson, who became a national hero.

**If I Had an Army**

"I am a soldier. I have done the white people all the harm I could. I have fought them, and fought them bravely. If I had an army, I yet would fight, and contend to the last. But . . . my people are all gone—I can do no more than weep over the Misfortunes of my nation. Once I could animate my warriors to battle, but I cannot animate the dead. . . . But my people are gone . . . your people have destroyed my nation . . ."

*William Weatherford, Chief of the Red Stick Creeks, 1814*

# The War of 1812

Even after American independence, the British maintained a presence in the eastern part of North America, and there was continued hostility between Britain and the United States. When the War of 1812 broke out between the two nations, Tecumseh was made a brigadier general in the British army and led many Indian warriors from different tribes in the war against the Americans.

Pushmataha responded by joining the Americans and leading hundreds of Choctaw warriors in decisive battles against the Red Stick Creeks, the Muscogees who had joined Tecumseh. Pushmataha then led his men in support of General Andrew Jackson's army against the British at the Battle of New Orleans in January 1815, the last battle of the war and a victory for the United States.

## Pressure Mounts

These military contributions by the Choctaws made them heroes to the white settlers of the Mississippi Territory. The whites passed resolutions in the Mississippi legislature honoring the Choctaws and acknowledging the great debt the people of Mississippi owed to them.

Other Southerners, however, were demanding Indian removal. After the War of 1812, American settlers poured onto the land west of Georgia, allowing Mississippi to gain statehood by 1817. European immigrants were flooding into the country and quickly heading to the frontier to become settlers. The pressures on the Indians were mounting.

Georgians, in particular, pointed to the promise the U.S. government had made in 1803. They resented Indian presence more than ever because their African-American slaves kept

White Georgians launched many attacks against Seminole villages such as this one. To their fury, the Georgians found that their runaway slaves had joined the Seminoles in their resistance to American invasion.

running off to Florida, where the Seminoles took them in and gave them protection from the Georgians.

## The Choctaw Treaty of 1820

In 1820, the United States got its loyal allies, the Choctaws, to agree to a **treaty** in which the U.S. government granted the Choctaws a huge area west of the Mississippi River in exchange for part of their remaining land in Mississippi. The Choctaws, however, retained the core of their Mississippi land and refused to consider moving to their new, western land as a whole tribe.

The Great **Seal** of the Choctaw nation has the design of a bow with three arrows, representing three great chiefs, and a pipe in the shape of a hatchet, representing the nation's governing council. The seal was used on official documents until the Choctaw nation was dissolved by the U.S. government in 1907.

Andrew Jackson (right) receives a tribute from voters during his campaign for the presidency in 1828. During Jackson's two terms as president, Native Americans were forced into nearly a hundred treaties that eroded their rights.

Eventually, the Americans forced the Choctaws to negotiate another treaty in 1825, removing their right to an area of remaining Choctaw land that white **squatters** had occupied.

## The Gold Rush and President Jackson

Two blows came in 1828. Georgians discovered gold in the far south of Cherokee country, on land also claimed by Georgia. The gold rush was in full swing there by 1829, and it was as wild and lawless as any in U.S. history. Georgians, eager to mine all of the gold, now had another compelling reason to demand removal.

Also in 1828, Andrew Jackson—hero of the frontier and the War of 1812—was elected president of the United States. Jackson had long argued for Indian removal. For the Five Civilized Tribes, their worst nightmare was about to come true. They were simply in the way, and the U.S. government was about to move them out of the way, no matter what the cost might be.

**Indefeasible Rights of Man**

"You will see [Americans] one hour lecturing their mob on the indefeasible [absolute and unchangeable] rights of man, and the next driving from their homes the children of the soil, whom they have bound themselves to protect by the most solemn treaties."

*Frances Trollope, visitor to the United States from England,*
*Domestic Manners of the Americans, 1832*

# Chapter 4

# On the Trail of Tears

The Five Civilized Tribes took different routes along the Trail of Tears to Indian Territory (in present-day Oklahoma). It was a long, wretched, and often fatal journey.

### The Indian Removal Act

With President Jackson's vigorous support, the U.S. Congress passed the Indian Removal Act on May 28, 1830. President Jackson praised Congress, calling the act "just and humane."

The five tribes were to be removed to the region that is now Oklahoma. In 1830, there was no such state as Oklahoma—the area was not even organized as Indian Territory until 1834. It was a wilderness, part of Arkansas Territory, and it was generally referred to as "the West." The Choctaws and Chickasaws would be sent into the southeastern region. The Cherokees would go into the northeastern part, and the Muscogees and Seminoles were allocated the east central region.

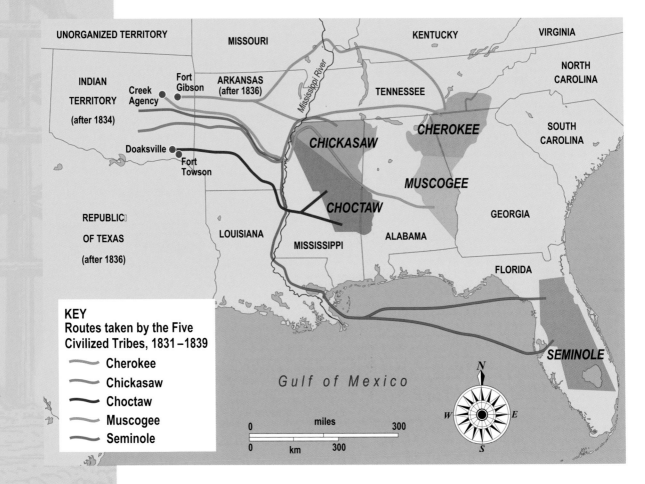

KEY
Routes taken by the Five
Civilized Tribes, 1831–1839
- Cherokee
- Chickasaw
- Choctaw
- Muscogee
- Seminole

# The Removal Treaties

Under the terms of the treaties made between the U.S. government and the Indians, the tribes owned the land to which they were being sent. In theory, any member of the five tribes could choose instead to receive an individual farm and remain in the Southeast. But in practice, U.S. officials simply refused to enroll anyone under those provisions, except for some tribal leaders who were bribed with large farms to get them to sign a treaty.

This treaty proclamation signed by President Martin van Buren in 1838 accompanied one of the many removal agreements forced on Indian tribes.

## The Choctaw Treaty
The United States decided that the best chance of getting the removal process going quickly would be with their old allies, the Choctaws, some of whom now understood that removal could not be avoided. A faction of the tribe negotiated the best terms they could in the Treaty of Dancing Rabbit Creek in 1830. This was the first of the removal treaties.

The treaty bitterly divided the Choctaws once more. Two large, armed groups confronted each other, but no shots were fired.

## The First Removal
Choctaw removal got underway in the winter of 1831–1832, with about four thousand Choctaws. A large removal was planned for each winter for three years until all of the Choctaws had been removed. Perhaps no one could have foreseen the high death toll that removal would bring.

The Choctaws became the first to experience the horror. Winter was thought to be the safest season from the terrible diseases of the nineteenth century, but it proved to be a deadly time for moving the very old and the very young. People had to travel several hundred miles in extreme cold. Many had to walk, most being barefoot. They were provided with inadequate food and clothing, only one thin blanket per person. Severe weather caused many to freeze to death, while others became fatally ill.

The first winter removal was undertaken by private **contractors** paid by the government with money owed to the five tribes. The groups being moved were mismanaged and got lost, wandering into swamps. At times, the Choctaws waded through water that was waist deep. When the travelers ran out of food as they reached Arkansas Territory, the non-Native people who lived there responded by raising the price of corn. It was a disaster, and when the surviving Choctaws finally reached the land in the West, many were so weak and sick that they soon died.

Choctaws traditionally smoked pipes to confirm agreements. When the Choctaws signed the Treaty of Dancing Rabbit Creek in 1830, they used this pipe bowl, handed down for hundreds of years in the Choctaw nation.

**Traveling Barefoot**

"[The Choctaws] walked for twenty-four hours barefoot through the snow and ice before reaching Vicksburg [Mississippi]."

*William S. Colquhoun, U.S. official conducting the Choctaw removal through Mississippi, 1831*

## Contractors and Costs

The U.S. government responded to the first winter removal by deciding that it had cost too much. It had not, however, cost the United States anything. The expenses of the removals were borne by the Indian tribes out of the proceeds of the sale of their tribal lands in the Southeast. (They didn't receive any actual money from the sales for many years.)

The United States decided to put the U.S. Army in charge of the removals. The army still had to rely on private contractors to provide food, clothing, and transportation for the Indians. That proved to be one of the most deadly flaws in the system. Dishonest contractors stole much of the money. They did this by buying cheap, thin blankets and keeping the profits; by delivering cheap, spoiled food to the supply points far ahead of time, so the army would not know how long it had been spoiled; and by other frauds that caused many deaths.

Even when fraud was not involved, communications between the U.S. Army and contractors were bad throughout all the removals. Food was delivered to the wrong places, and large

### Human Suffering

"This unexpected cold weather must produce much human suffering. Our poor emigrants, many of them quite naked, and without shelter, must suffer, it is impossible to do otherwise; and my great fears are that many of them will get frosted."

*Captain Jacob Brown, U.S. Army, conducting the Choctaw removal through Arkansas Territory, 1832*

This painting by Troy Anderson shows people on the Trail of Tears in winter. Many lost their lives to the freezing weather.

groups of Indians were taken on the wrong routes where there was no food or shelter.

## Second and Third Choctaw Removals

With the Indians in a weakened condition, sickness and disease proved deadly. The second winter removal of about 6,000

Pushmataha, pictured here, had opposed Tecumseh and led the Choctaws in support of the United States in the War of 1812. In the 1820s and 1830s, however, Pushmataha tried unsuccessfully to resist the removal of his people.

Choctaws in 1832 to 1833, although managed better by the army, coincided with a devastating epidemic of **cholera**. The death toll was even higher than that of the first removal.

Only about 1,000 Choctaws could be induced to move during the third winter, leaving about 6,000 landless Choctaws in Mississippi. Most of them eventually made their way west on their own over the next few decades.

Of 11,000 Choctaws who were moved, 2,500

died during removal or shortly afterward, when sickness and starvation took their toll. Sadly, the removal of the Choctaws would set a tragic pattern for the later removals.

## Chickasaw Removal

Even after he knew the full horror of removal, President Andrew Jackson forged ahead with the process, determined to see it through with the other tribes. A Chickasaw removal treaty—the Treaty of Ponotoc—was negotiated in 1832, but it had to be amended in 1834 before the Chickasaws would agree to move.

Having learned of the horror of the Choctaw removals, the Chickasaws insisted on providing many of their own wagons and a lot of their own supplies. Most of them—about 4,000 people—were removed in 1837, in smaller groups and earlier in the year than the Choctaws had been. Rains turned the journey into a nightmare of

The Chickasaw people endured removal in 1837. The figure of the ancient warrior on the Chickasaw Great Seal both symbolizes the courage of the Chickasaw people and honors Tishomingo, last of the great war chiefs before the Chickasaws were removed.

### Burying a Child in Stranger-Land

"She could only carry her dying child in her arms a few miles farther, and then, she must stop in a stranger-land and consign her much loved babe to the cold ground, and that without pomp or ceremony, and pass on with the multitude. . . . When I passed the last detachment of those suffering exiles and thought that my native countrymen had thus expelled them from their native soil and their much loved homes . . . I turned from the sight with feelings which language cannot express and wept like childhood then."

*An American traveler who saw the Cherokee removal in Missouri, 1839*

The plow and sheaf of wheat in the Great Seal of the Muscogeee nation are symbols of farming. The Muscogees were known for their agricultural skills before they were aggressively removed in the winter of 1836–1837.

mud and sickness, and about 600 Chickasaws died of smallpox while being moved through Arkansas (which in 1836 had become a state to the east of Indian Territory).

## Muscogee Removal

The Muscogee removal treaty was negotiated in 1832, but many of the tribal members were unhappy with it. Before removals could get underway, greedy whites swarmed into the Muscogee homeland and literally kicked many people out of their homes.

When some Muscogees met the intruders with violence, the U.S. Army sent troops to move the Muscogees by force. In 1836, nearly 15,000 people were rounded up. About 2,500 of them, classified as **hostiles**, were put in chains and marched to the West during the winter of 1836–1837, a journey that killed hundreds of Muscogees. The remaining people were hastily removed under such horrible conditions that 3,500 of those who survived removal were so weakened by it that they died within a year.

## Seminole Removal

In 1832, a faction of the Seminoles negotiated a removal treaty, the Treaty of Payne's Landing. Some Seminoles left Florida, traveling by boat to Louisiana and then heading north. Many people refused to be removed, however, and fought the Americans for years.

## The Seminole Wars

Led by Osceola, Wildcat, and former slave John Horse, large numbers of Seminoles stayed in Florida and fought against removal. One thousand U.S. soldiers were sent in to remove the Seminoles by force but were defeated. More troops were sent, and the Seminoles fled to the Everglades of southern Florida, where they held out against the Americans.

The toll on the U.S. Army soon became staggering—it was the most costly Indian war in U.S. history, both in money and soldiers. By 1842, three thousand Seminoles had been captured and removed by force. The wars had cost $20 million (hundreds of millions of dollars today) as well as the life of one American soldier for every two Seminoles removed. The United States simply gave up and left the remaining few hundred Seminoles in the Everglades.

Osceola, the great Seminole leader.

John Ross led the Cherokees who resisted removal under a treaty that did not represent the wishes of the majority. Ross ended up being forced to move, however, along with thousands of other Cherokees.

## Cherokee Removal

A small minority of the Cherokees, led by Major Ridge, his son John Ridge, and Elias Boudinot, signed the Treaty of New Echota in 1835 and were removed to the West. The large majority of Cherokees, however, under Chief John Ross, refused to acknowledge the removal treaty.

In 1838, the U.S. Army swept into the Cherokee nation with seven thousand troops and rounded up most of the Cherokees. Thousands of people were held in prison camps under terrible conditions until the removal got underway.

The Cherokee Trail of Tears became the most **infamous** of all the removals, mostly because by that time the tragedy of the situation had, at last, attracted the attention of the American people. Many white Americans, mostly from northern states, protested against the

**Dragged from Their Homes**

"Men working in the fields were arrested and driven to the **stockades**. Women were dragged from their homes by soldiers whose language they could not understand. Children were often separated from their parents and driven into the stockades with the sky for a blanket and the earth for a pillow. And often the old and the infirm were prodded with bayonets to hasten them to the stockade."

*Private John G. Burnett, a U.S. Army soldier who participated in the Cherokee removal*

policy, but without success. Most of the Cherokees were removed at one time, during the winter of 1838–1839, in thirteen groups of about 1,000 each. The death toll was about 4,000 people, including those who had died back in the prison camps.

By the end of the decade, thousands of members of the Five Civilized Tribes had suffered an experience so shattering that it was an open question whether or not they would ever be able to recover. About 60,000 southeastern Indians were moved to the West, at a cost of about 15,000 lives.

**No Hope**

"We are in trouble, Sir, our hearts are very heavy. . . . We have no hope unless you will help us . . . we ask that you not send us . . . at this time of year. If you do we shall die, our wives will die or our children will die. . . "

*Petition of one hundred prominent Cherokees to General Winfield Scott, 1838*

The removal of the Cherokees killed nearly one-third of the 13,000 people sent along the Cherokee Trail of Tears. In all, one-quarter of the people removed from their home-lands never made it to the West or died soon after arriving.

# After Removal

## Origin Stories

Four of the Five Civilized Tribes have origin stories telling of a time, long ago, when they came to the Southeast from a land far away to the west. Some of the tribal elders tried to make the removals more bearable by saying that perhaps the Native people were returning to their old homelands. The idea was not much help in easing the pain and suffering of removal.

## Life and Death in a New Land

In the first few years, life in the new land proved almost as deadly as the removals had been. At the end of the Trail of Tears, despite treaties guaranteeing their support, many people found themselves simply dumped in an uninhabited region without food, clothing, or shelter.

There was no housing provided for the thousands of people who arrived in Indian Territory. But those who survived removal were eventually able to build homes for their families. This house belonged to the Cherokee Sequoyah, who had negotiated with the U.S. government for his people's removal from Arkansas.

After arriving in the West, the five tribes were still at the mercy of the U.S. government. Sometimes food supplies arrived and were handed out in rations, as shown here. Most agreements to provide essential supplies, however, were not honored.

For agricultural peoples uprooted from their farms and transplanted into a wilderness, starvation was the first enemy that had to be faced. The U.S. government had obligated itself to provide food and other necessities for a year after removal. But corruption in the government resulted in some men, serving as Indian agents, buying up barrels of spoiled meat cheaply and pocketing the surplus money themselves. Others were honest men who tried their best to help the exiled tribes as much as they could. Without the food or farming equipment that had been promised, however, the people of the Five Civilized Tribes continued to die.

## Tension Among Tribes

The Seminoles were not happy when they were removed to the Muscogee

**Failures Without End**

"I am here starving with the Chickasaws by gross mismanagement on the part of the contractors, and when our situation will be bettered is hard for me to tell, for it is one failure after another without end."

*William R. Guy, a U.S. official with the Chickasaws in Indian Territory, 1838*

land in the West and told that they must join the Muscogee nation. They had been a separate tribe far too long to be willing to do that. Neither group was happy with the arrangement, and tensions ran high between the Muscogees and the Seminoles.

Likewise, the Chickasaws were not happy about being told that they must join the Choctaw nation. The Chickasaws simply refused to leave the camps where the U.S. Army had placed them, and they demanded their own nation.

For the Cherokees, matters proved far more deadly. The rift in their nation over the removal treaty had not healed. The majority of the Cherokees who suffered removal on the Trail of Tears viewed the Cherokees who had signed the removal treaty as traitors. Once in the West, Major Ridge, Elias Boudinot, and other Cherokees who had signed the treaty were assassinated. The violence only deepened the divisions between the two factions.

## New Constitutions

Despite losing thousands of their people during the first few years, the tribes were able to survive. They wrote new **constitutions** for their governments, modeled after the U.S. Constitution. They organized school systems for their children. People cleared farmland, planted crops, and began bringing order and stability back into their lives.

Once they had recovered from the removal, the five tribes entered into a golden age for their nations—golden, at least, in comparison to the horrors they had been put through. During that period, they were pretty much left alone by outsiders. Both the Seminoles and the Chickasaws negotiated treaties that allowed them to form their own separate nations.

**Cherokee Alphabet.**

| | | | | | |
|---|---|---|---|---|---|
| D $a$ | R $e$ | T $i$ | Ꮼ $o$ | O $u$ | i $v$ |
| S $ga$ O $ka$ | F $ge$ | Y $gi$ | A $go$ | J $gu$ | E $gv$ |
| Ꮺ $ha$ | P $he$ | Ꮑ $hi$ | F $ho$ | Γ $hu$ | Ꮚ $hv$ |
| W $la$ | Ꮄ $le$ | P $li$ | G $lo$ | M $lu$ | Ꮎ $lv$ |
| Ꮖ $ma$ | Ol $me$ | H $mi$ | Ꮝ $mo$ | Ꭹ $mu$ | |
| Ꮎ $na$ Ꮏ $hna$ G $nah$ | Ꮄ $ne$ | h $ni$ | Z $no$ | Ꮕ $nu$ | O $nv$ |
| Ꮏ $qua$ | Ꮗ $que$ | Ꮖ $qui$ | Ꮴ $quo$ | Ꮖ $quu$ | Ꮛ $quv$ |
| U $sa$ Ꮝ $s$ | Ꮞ $se$ | b $si$ | Ꮭ $so$ | Ꮽ $su$ | R $sv$ |
| Ꮣ $da$ W $ta$ | Ꮝ $de$ Ꮦ $te$ | Ꮩ $di$ Ꮧ $ti$ | V $do$ | S $du$ | Ꮿ $dv$ |
| Ꮪ $dla$ Ꮫ $tla$ | L $tle$ | C $tli$ | Ꮶ $tlo$ | Ꮲ $tlu$ | P $tlv$ |
| G $tsa$ | V $tse$ | Ir $tsi$ | K $tso$ | J $tsu$ | C $tsv$ |
| G $wa$ | Ꮿ $we$ | Ꮻ $wi$ | Ꮼ $wo$ | Ꮽ $wu$ | 6 $wv$ |
| Ꮿ $ya$ | B $ye$ | Ꮵ $yi$ | Ꮿ $yo$ | G $yu$ | B $yv$ |

Cherokee schools taught the alphabet created by Sequoyah that is still used today. Each sound made in speech is represented by one of eighty-five symbols, or "talking leaves." The Cherokee nation adopted the alphabet in 1821.

### The Seminoles after Removal

"Among the poor, neglected and despised Seminoles, there is as much honor and integrity as among any other tribe. . . . They have great affection for their children; pay much deference to their wives; and when at home in their families, appear to appreciate the enjoyments of the domestic circle . . . and it would tend to produce this result if they had a country they could call their own."

*Thomas L. Judge, Seminole agent, Muscogee Nation, Indian Territory, August 26, 1844*

General Stand Watie, a supporter of slavery, led the Cherokees who joined the Confederates in the Civil War. He had signed the Cherokee removal treaty that bitterly divided the nation.

In Indian Territory, as it was now called, farms responded to the newcomers' care and skills, and herds of cattle, horses, and hogs grew to be plentiful. The tribes were allowed to govern themselves without interference from the outside world.

## The Civil War

All of that changed with the outbreak of the American Civil War in 1861. Ignoring its promises to provide protection to the Indians, the United States immediately pulled all of its troops out of the region, leaving the Five Civilized Tribes defenseless. They had no choice but to negotiate treaties with the **Confederates**. Because of those treaties, the United States would view the tribes as defeated enemies after the war, even though the war in fact divided the tribes in much the same way as it divided U.S. citizens.

Both northern and southern armies swept through the Indian Territory, confiscating everything to feed their armies. The land of the Cherokee and Muscogee nations became bloody battlefields in the war. The people of those nations fled, some north to Kansas, some south to the Choctaws. But the armies of both sides ransacked those areas for food and livestock, too. The Indian death toll was high during the Civil War, but most deaths were caused by disease and **malnutrition**.

Members of the Five Civilized Tribes fought on both sides during the Civil War. One Cherokee,

General Stand Watie, rose to high rank and, in 1865, was the last Confederate general to surrender.

## After the Civil War

When the war was over, the United States negotiated treaties with all the tribes that allowed American railroads to pass through their nations. Within only a few years, floods of white settlers entered the Indian nations on those railroads. By the 1870s, Natives were outnumbered by Americans three to one in their own countries.

The whites began clamoring to abolish the Indian nations and form a state in Indian Territory. Congress assisted their efforts by passing laws requiring each Indian to accept an individual farm in private ownership, called an **allotment**. All remaining Indian land would then be thrown open to white settlement.

In 1907, the state of Oklahoma was created, and members of the Five Civilized Tribes were forced to become citizens of the new state. The guarantee that they would have their own nations in the West was not honored by the United States. Members of the Five Civilized Tribes could only watch helplessly as their nations were dissolved and their land was taken from them.

**A Promise Broken**

". . . no territory or state shall ever have a right to pass laws for the government of the Choctaw Nation of Red People and their descendants; and no part of the land granted them shall ever be embraced in any territory or state. . . ."

*Government of the United States, Article IV, Choctaw Removal Treaty of 1830*

In 1893, the U.S. government offered millions of acres of Indian Territory to white settlers. This photograph was taken as homesteaders, who had been waiting at the border, raced in to claim land that legally belonged to the Cherokees.

# Conclusion

These are the government headquarters of the removed Chickasaw people in Oklahoma, who are trying to maintain their traditions and gain legal rights for their nation.

## Oklahoma Tribes Reform Their Governments

When a national wave of Indian protest in the 1970s brought attention to Native problems, the tribes in Oklahoma were finally allowed to reform tribal governments. The Five Civilized Tribes each wrote new constitutions and elected tribal governments for the first time since statehood. Those tribal governments are now in conflict with the state of Oklahoma and the **federal** government, trying to regain many of the ordinary powers of government.

### A Heavy Weight

"The history of the Cherokee removal of 1838 . . . may well exceed in weight of grief and pathos any other passage in American history."

*James Mooney,* Historical Sketch of the Cherokee, *1900*

## Those Who Stayed Behind

Early in the twentieth century, the U.S. government became aware that there were pockets of southeastern Indians who had avoided removal and whose descendants remained in the Southeast. Most had been living, hardly noticed, on the fringes of southern society in swamps and other remote and unwanted areas.

The U.S. government started buying parcels of real estate so that those Indians might have some tribally owned land again. By the middle of the century, the Choctaws living in Mississippi were able to organize a government, write a constitution, and gain federal recognition as the Mississippi Band of Choctaw Indians. Other eastern bands of the Five Civilized Tribes also emerged. They include the eastern Cherokees near Cherokee, North Carolina, the Seminoles in southern Florida, and the Poarch Creeks and Mowa Choctaws in Alabama.

# The Legacy of the Trail of Tears

There was nothing inevitable about Indian removal. There was nothing that meant that it had to happen. It was a choice that was made by the American people of that generation. The Trail of Tears, and its aftermath, remains one of the most tragic and destructive events in the history of the Cherokees, Choctaws, Chickasaws, Muscogees, and Seminoles. It is also one of the cruelest episodes in the treatment of the original inhabitants of the North American continent by the U.S. government and the American people.

Some traditions survive—Cherokee elders continue to make baskets as their ancestors did.

The Trail of Tears resulted in the Five Civilized Tribes losing their land in the Southeast, and it cost the lives of about one-fourth of their people. Many of those people who died were the old people, the elders who possessed the cultural knowledge of their tribes. A great amount of cultural knowledge died with those elders, and there was no way to regain it.

# Time Line

| | |
|---:|:---|
| **1700s** | Some Muscogees move to Florida and form Seminole tribe. |
| **1747–1750** | Choctaw Civil War. |
| **1754–1763** | French and Indian War. |
| **1776–1783** | American Revolutionary War. |
| **1802** | President Thomas Jefferson makes first mention of Indian Removal. |
| **1803** | Louisiana Purchase. |
| | April 23: U.S. government promises Georgia to abolish Indian land titles in the state. |
| **1811** | Tecumseh attempts to form military alliance among southern tribes. |
| **1812–1815** | War of 1812. |
| **1820** | Treaty of 1820, in which Choctaws acquire land west of the Mississippi River. |
| **1825** | Choctaw Treaty of 1825 modifies Treaty of 1820. |
| **1828** | Georgians discover gold in Cherokee country and gold rush begins. |
| | Andrew Jackson is elected President of United States. |
| **1830** | Congress passes Indian Removal Act. |
| | Treaty of Dancing Rabbit Creek (Choctaw removal treaty). |
| **1831–1832** | First Choctaw removal begins Trail of Tears. |
| **1832** | Treaty of Ponotoc (Chickasaw removal treaty). |
| | Muscogee removal treaty. |
| | Treaty of Payne's Landing (Seminole removal treaty). |
| **1832–33** | Second Choctaw removal. |
| **1833–34** | Third Choctaw removal. |
| **1834** | Indian Territory is officially organized. |
| | Partial Seminole removal. |
| **1836** | Muscogee removal. |
| **1837** | Chickasaw removal. |
| **1838–39** | Cherokee removal. |
| **1861–1865** | American Civil War. |
| **1870s** | Railroads bring great numbers of white settlers to Indian Territory. |
| **1880s** | Congress begins forcing tribes in Indian Territory to accept individual allotments. |
| **1907** | Oklahoma becomes a state and Indian nations in Indian Territory are abolished. |

# Glossary

**allotment:** small area of farmland allocated to an individual or household.

**arbor:** shelter made of branches and leaves.

**cholera:** highly infectious disease that affects the intestine and that can kill large numbers of people when an epidemic breaks out.

**clan:** division of a tribe consisting of small group that has a duty to provide services, such as burials, for its members, as well as many other social functions.

**colony:** settlement, area, or country owned or controlled by another nation.

**Confederate:** having to do with the southern states—and their people and soldiers—that broke away from the United States during the American Civil War.

**constitution:** basic rules of government for a nation.

**contractor:** person given a contract, or agreement, to perform a service for a fee.

**economic:** having to do with the production and distribution of goods and services.

**effigy:** image representing a person or an animal.

**federal:** having to do with the whole nation rather than separate states.

**frontier:** edge of something known or settled. The U.S. frontier moved west across North America as white settlement expanded.

**hostile:** unfriendly. The U.S. government termed as "hostiles" all Indians who resisted white control or settlement.

**infamous:** famous in a bad way, such as a terrible event or person.

**malnutrition:** state of ill health caused by not getting enough nutritious food.

**nation:** the people of a particular country, which in Indian terms means a large tribe; also refers to the geographical territory established by a tribe or other group of people.

**nomadic:** traveling around as a way of life rather than living in one place; in the case of Native Americans, usually to follow herds of big game animals.

**policy:** plan or way of doing things that is decided upon in advance and then used in managing situations or making decisions.

**republic:** nation led by a leader or group of officials chosen by the citizens and in which citizens have a voice in how they are governed.

**seal:** stamp bearing an official symbol of a government or nation.

**squatter:** person who lives on land without permission of the landowners.

**stockade:** enclosed area that is usually surrounded by thick wooden posts and used for holding prisoners.

**territory:** land claimed by a particular group. Regions such as Arkansas Territory and Indiana Territory in the 1800s were claimed and governed by the United States but were not included in any actual states.

**treaty:** agreement between two groups or nations after negotiation, often at the end of a period of conflict.

# Further Information

## Books

Bruchac, Joseph. *The Journal of Jesse Smoke: A Cherokee Boy. Trail of Tears, 1838* (My Name Is America). Scholastic, 2001.

Collier, Christopher and James Lincoln Collier. *Andrew Jackson's America: 1824–1850* (Drama of American History). Benchmark, 1998.

Connell, Kate. *These Lands Are Ours: Tecumseh's Fight for the Old Northwest.* Raintree/Steck-Vaughn, 1993.

Santella, Andrew. *The Cherokee* (True Books: American Indians). Children's Press, 2000.

Sonder, Ben. *Osceola, Patriot and Warrior* (Stories of America). Raintree/Steck-Vaughn, 1992.

## Web Sites

**www.choctawnation.com** Official web site of the Choctaw nation offers historical information about the tribe.

**www.nps.gov/trte/** National Park Service site for the Trail of Tears National Historic Park, which has preserved parts of the Cherokee Trail of Tears and sites along the way.

**www.rosecity.net/tears/** Tourist web site offers information about the Trail of Tears and lots of relevant links.

## Useful Addresses

**National Trail of Tears Association**
1110 North University, Suite 143
Little Rock, AR 72207
Telephone: (501) 666-9032

# Index

Page numbers in *italics* indicate maps and diagrams. Page numbers in **bold** indicate other illustrations.